JW ATTERBURY VOL.1

LOUD, SILENT, THOUGHTS

BY

JOEL WASHINGTON ATTERBURY

Special dedication

TISHA BOWEN

My cousin Tisha who has always been like a sister to me. Appreciate your outlook on things when we speak especially when people of dark energy want to dim my light source and bring me to the evil side of thought because of their insecurities.

Everything isn't always everything, yet all that is probably is lol.

Love you always cuz!

ACKNOWLEDGEMENT

To my cousin Lydia Dowling who always know what she knows when we speak on things.

Always enjoy our crazy conversations LOL.

But I appreciate you always checking in with me and giving support.

Thank you for always being who you are and nothing less.

Love you

King Atterberry Ink

Copyrighted © 2022 Library of Congress.

Published by: Joel Washington Atterbury

ISBN: 979-8-9861071-3-4

Contact Information

Email: kingatterberry7@gmail.com

Facebook: Joel Washington Atterbury

Instagram: king_atterberry_ink

Contents

JW ATTERBURY

Eagles never speak

Soaring through the mist on a wish without a dream.

Destination unseen I always land where I want to.

Flight patterns observed no muscle on the rescue.

Always keep me free within clouds of true hope.

Some of y'all looking as if you waiting on my failure.

Whatever suit you I'm neutral I move with force.

Let me speak about the course ok I been on many tracks.

If the heart attracts don't stab my back, I'm the JW living.

Breathing and eating only nap to rest my physical.

Rise again against the wind my wing and claws kinetic.

Seasons lie inside the weather whether it be or not.

It's not the spot or the slot that feed mouths that drop.

Move baby move

Arms extended wide come inside the introduction.

May I tell you something nice that will keep your mind alert.

Fifty-one years on earth my compassion remains high.

Allow my aura to illuminate within your lovely spirit.

You speak and I know, feeling as if we're close together.

The eyes open a smile that take place upon our journey.

It's the look outside a language that's understood.

Kiss the time we both share appreciate what's in the air.

Touch the place that's been abandoned with a healthy balance.

Adjusting my own story, it's the challenge that is remarkable.

So, when that shadow diminishes, and that image is no more.

Here's part of me for your core feel the allure just know I got you.

Enter your outside

How does it feel when your reflection looks different in the mirror.

Sound of your voice is unclear because of toxic interactions.

What happened to compassion now that the laughing is gone.

Can't hear with your ears so now I speak with my eyes.

Imagine being a image inside a glass broken frame.

Who all will be the blame for not hanging the picture up.

Been walked into the unknown chose a path upon a route.

As long I get to where I'm going, I refuse to be stuck.

Never one that's questioned lessons are in a briefcase.

Harlem got a toothpaste the smile is in style, hello.

Salutes are being given while some keep on forgetting.

If I am my father's father, I'm not changing what's missing.

Purification

She said her mind was made up with travel plans made.

Left many memories that I discarded from my mind.

Only peace can release what can be heavy after a while.

I found answers speaking to water we are bonded by clarity.

Doesn't matter the condition from pulsations I listen.

My only new beginnings are consistent with honest thoughts.

Now that I walk inside a presence of two men who are deceased.

Heart rate is back normal there are no hands on my clock.

Whatever time wanted to say only the sky reveals to me.

Change that come and go only sight can move intentions.

For the seen and administered deep within.

The audible orchestra conducted by me is given free.

Ocean due

We met between the moon and the sun riding a star.

Didn't know about each other until our paths crossed fast.

First was the glimpse although molecular exchange was there.

At that point celestial powers began to grow within our body.

That event brought forth a consciousness inside of our galaxy.

Moving around a universe that connected both our auras.

Hard to explain where do we fall amongst the unknown.

Dropping down upon this planet as an earth and I am a god.

Enlightening stood upon one phase of our stage.

There's a cycle underway were holding on for a tomorrow.

Entering inside of one another as a strong anomaly.

We won't ever be understood because we're outside of nature.

Up and up

There's only room to explore what we came here for.

It's the findings beyond internal reach now the hands touch matters.

Solutions are in place to bring forth brighter days.

Let us all get use to something better and greater than before.

No longer are we stagnant the movement is on the rise.

Distraction is at an all-time high ignore the foolishness.

Separate go getters from temporary puppet masters.

Procrastinated elevators still can't find the right floor.

Speak things into existence allow light into your life.

So broken shadows shaky grounds are hard to walk on.

My warmth stay positioned without ever being regulated.

No strings attached hard to match compass where your love at.

Manifestation 1

Shark skin shoes on stepping out that great white.

Got a date late night afterwards space flight.

Unknown destination this occasion is a situation.

What we facing is an open vessel operation.

Navigate around the physical with my vehicle.

My lady mind is in another place she knows how I do.

Imagery on point handy with her fixtures.

Two shots of clear nothing brown get the picture.

Inhaling her air as she exhales breathing fast.

Forgotten is the past of her last so I laugh.

Syndical grin while my eyes look in hers.

This only occurred because I'm what she prefers.

Fresh on the cakes while I taste which is safe.

As the heart race my hands trace the beauty of her face.

Back to life we soul to soul allowing spirit to control.

Wherever we may go know-one else could ever troll.

It's a natural creative view built for the loving view.

Enjoying what is built for two never mind what's ridiculed.

Manifestation 2

After this weekend of work while working just to work.

My chill moment is having time to self-digressing hours.

While healthcare is changing be aware of your health care.

Because the same thing that's Payed attention can affect you.

Relax inside your armor watching the tube without the news.

Documentaries and comedies can change your life narrative.

Laugh and smile outside of feelings where thoughts can go deep.

The heart is not hard to reach so be mindful of your intake.

Make the next day your fun day no matter what's going on.

Some folks still get it wrong going mad what an injustice.

Interact with what's beautiful that's soothing to your conscious.

Leave behind nonsense that shake your grounding balance.

Showtime

Anywhere that I go find water fix my eyes on.

There's only one creator I rely on when I'm sky born.

As well have a high on life it's a place I live in.

When I return it's the beginning coming back fetal position.

These thoughts cross my mind as I watch ocean waves.

Opportunity of a good day is where I don't lay.

Sand on my flip flops never like the open toes.

As the sun beams on me I'm feeling remarkable.

So, in or out state give me a beach with no chair.

Standing like a soldier of society with no gear.

Only chest to bear with shorts on and beverages.

This is my spirit medicine you know how diabetes is.

Looking at chance directly my hope on faith recycled.

Even if I don't try to accommodate, I might do.

Something special as head back onto land.

One thing I understand is I am a man of circumstance.

JW ATTERBURY

Easy beloved

Now that the focus is back, and the jewels are dropped.

King will drop in any slot just to fill that spot.

Pay comedians no mind my time is very precious.

Waking up every morning preparing a nice breakfast.

So, your bagel coffee people in your cubicle office.

Don't let them phone calls or emails make you nauseous.

I run with laborers mixed employees in a union.

Outside of that profession I know what I be doing.

Feeding the culture crafting poems on different shows.

With some last dragon action with a Leroy glow.

Phenomenal guests spitting wide audience listen.

King has a vision that's why I stay on a mission.

Hosting, content creating while evolving.

The hate is so real in the world that hold problems.

How do we support what's lost in bigger thoughts.

My favorite super sport is to find a super force.

Blind truth

Came from two parents that loved each other deep.

Many times, they couldn't see one another but me.

So, I learned from both in many ways they displayed.

Their honesty was framed in a portrait well displayed.

Walking into unknown matters life is a mystery.

Formulated my own legacy my kids know the history.

No need to tell my story when I'm gone right or wrong.

Search through all my books there are psalms in my poems.

Some waters murky and others clear as blue skies.

I haven't left yet so hello instead of goodbye.

Conflicted spirits wanna compromise the route in which I walk on.

There's a song that king sing beware of open folded arms.

Narrative of a hope rider I'm a ghostwriter to my own self.

Never feeling myself there's no one else so watch out when asking for help.

Backstabbing is critical main goal is to get rid of you.

Situations are like horse glue beware of clown's fools.

I AM....

I am an original who see through the differences of troubled societies.

I am a Blackman standing on the shoulders of my ancestors.

I am truth looking at the liars of injustice thoughts.

I am the scissors cutting the strings off the puppet masters dolls.

I am the strength moving in circles that see the weak taken advantage of.

I am the curve that don't answer to manipulators and opportunist.

I am the bell that ring like twelve on a Sunday you know what time it is.

I am the child of two people that gave life to a guardian.

I am the writer the poet the author the creative content
maker without distraction.

I am the pen that hit the pad with a rhyme scheme or
manifesting iLL words spoken.

I am the gentleman that open opportunity willingly holding humility.

I am a timekeeper projecting direction without tardiness.

I am the energy within an energy that carry a life force.

I am the power source connecting to a tribe outlet.

I am the input to a story so grand beyond my plans.

I am the newest rendition of the man behind my father's hands.

GALLOTRON IS BACK!! Check the archive!

Pray for something

Where is the fork in the road upon the story that's told.

Some hungry for the pot of gold wherever it's sold.

Higher my ambition the vision is hard wired.

Never rider with liars I'm watching the time expire.

Enjoying the unexpected resurrect ways of a past life.

Too many involved and super hype I suggest you hold on tight.

Grounds I walk on supposed to be leveled and steady.

Blessings already coming heavy I'm building levees.

Temperature changing as the season start breathing.

Mentality of reason kill the thoughts that were grieving.

So of course, bed rest is comfortable on my left crest.

Wake up the next morning feeling fresh as money pressed.

Cards on the table

If I showed all my hands and expressed all my plans.

Moved to another state inexpensive place changing my pay rate.

Get involved with what's new appreciate my just due.

Would I be the same man that you all once knew.

Reserve choice of action my gratitude no attitude.

Enjoying an altitude sitting on clouds with better view.

From upstairs it looks so nice within these fresh heights.

Writing on a terrace or balcony I'm all for it.

Differences in demeanor the stress level is vague.

Why wouldn't I wanna stay from a long time of charades.

People places and things I see life in many spectrums.

Light shine so bright inside my aura god warn them.

Name the name that change with better outcome.

Strange is strained lower the pain the reach got him.

The love is hard when the vibe connects differently.

They attack my mobility I acquired an inability.

Flawed!

Only natural

You said I couldn't have you but here's a question that I ask you.

What does it take to move your spirit to align with mine.

Is it the words that I speak that I place action behind.

Or the little things that I do when I am exploring your mind.

May I whisper in your ear something to clear the air.

Can I bring you to place that I keep secret far but near.

It's the personality of my fondest honest thoughts.

Sent from a true and living heart that only wish to start.

While I look inside your eyes and smile hard just because.

What can become a different love after a buzz.

An idea can appear from what's expressed beyond the chest.

A beautiful union can be formed with happiness when souls connect.

With no expectation high I only want a piece of you.

First the mental then the physical if we bond that's passion fruit.

As one we become the meaning of fun when we begin.

Start as friends and then began a relationship that win.

Lover

Let me hold on to what me and you never thought would happen.

Allow time to move our days and bring to life a new caption.

It's his and her aura closely combined mixed with days.

That right there is a wave where we can go at a steady pace.

Once I look at you, I snapshot the image of your lips, nose, and eyes.

I know that I am reaching but my words can run pass the lines.

See I consider you to be what I need without a mystery.

Unification of a man and a woman that's called synergy.

Your fine features killing me so delightful have me licking my lips.

Just once one wish allows me to get to scratch that itch.

I know you may have dealt with them, but I am a new beginning.

Reintroduce recalibrated from a station where there's no playing.

If all bases are loaded let me knock, chances out the park.

Bring a light source to your life force protecting you from the dark.

Understand communication while trial and error wait around.

Find balance in between the here and now make it a style.

So, I wonder if I can taste the vegetables on you.

Accommodate the thought of having something fine and so special.

Fearless

What the world doesn't realize is many of us are defiant.

Beating out the odds that are stacked against the workers.

And when I say workers, I mean those who work hard.

To overcome adversities of the ones who are in charge.

So, I say please respect mines as I respect yours respectfully.

The duality of choices made are poisoned by the madness.

Life is just a year full of four seasons of breathing.

Sometimes we're grieving having tough times believing.

So, I pray against the monster of selfishness it's effortless.

Moments I close my ears to the nonsense that's presented.

Energy of my pendant's some are raw, and some are charmed.

This is just a psalm from off JW'S crested arm.

Bear a cross with red ink in its words to a sentence.

Lined across a white page mentally I finish.

Never mind some quotable things that I am speaking.

I refuse to give up, so I get up and move my good foot.

Kick trouble in the ass for the laugh trapping my past.

Camouflage my mask underneath whatever's bad.

Bring my dreams into fruition from hope, love, and life.

Gamble that the price is right when the world is sacrificed.

Beyond the vibe

Over sounds that embody the physical changing the frequency frequently
mentally opening channels the beauty is special when holding a appetite
ready to nicely indulge filling the hunger to write.

What's motion without movement I'm doing something that's natural no
need to ask you I'm the cool straight out the Frigidaire.

Appear as a feeling or emotion this a token for a free pass flow through
waves like sea bass highlighting without the strobe flash.

Hands grip a sandwich that's made from top grade enjoy your hoagie I'm the
dark liquor man smoking stogies, so we adapt to lounges that fill air with
many tunes I consume what's in the room enjoying all that loom.

Grateful for gestures of kindness from like-mindedness took off invisible
blinders the opts can see the stature that stand on gods will as I peel back
the covers of evil within the people Skylab's waiting on heroes.

Returns are awesome without a cost out of pocket while writing on margins
what's the spread whatever's led to accomplish a mission with no division
while I'm living off playing position, I'm happy now that I listen.

If old is new from elders my generation are settlers of granting moments
between what was then I found the now raising the stakes creating a
powerful unity, it's the beauty of grouping a crew or posse let's get it
together.

DIVINE TIMING

Nine point one

You don't want a problem with this Washington.

Who don't mix and blend with those friends that trend.

I'm the truth who some admire judged by the liars.

I move through air on wires my connect the flyest.

Jokers break your center piece words get filthy.

I'm from the old Harlem but reside in south Jersey.

Never caught up in that gutter ish got a chick loving lip.

Kiss her with the lines I spit baby just loving it.

Please hug the comfort, zones are innocent.

Of course, there's a benefit my dad son is living it.

Killing it, special with that four five.

Running off vibes that make haters look and hide.

Place where I reside between could've, would've, should've.

Best version of me is to rise above empathy.

Walk within the highest form of being who I am today.

You can have a better day if you can find a way.

Manifest my last name into a fortune of fame.

The change came and rained on a dry up terrain.

Inhale my air

Your smile tells a story when I am looking in your eyes.

The back and forth is special sharing honesty and care.

As my heart speak in motion dear diva where you been.

This is only the beginning of what's next to come.

Sound of music that we share builds a bond around our time.

Even a early morning greeting set the tone of our day.

Simplicity of our conversations creates a world where we can chill.

Appreciation beyond the outer existence explains what we are doing.

Do we go back or move forward maybe take charge of circumstance.

How about taking a chance while our thoughts continue to dance.

With high fever on our meter what is this just let it grow.

As we are walking on this path, we already know our role.

Play feign

Ayo, I break down the walls in halls tear up floors.

Therefore, conversations in back doors are put on stalls.

By law stand against the insecurity fault

Male or females the details are flawed.

Of course, I move around waste check your own place.

Not up for debate I create with godly traits.

I am who I be JW Atterbury.

There's no adversary's so me and her don't worry.

Ink slide across lines page without rage.

Lion out the cage walking inside his wave.

Okay this is just a letter to the watchers.

Blasphemous commentators waiting just to mark us.

The mane stays freshly groomed but get fiery.

Recheck your journal notepad or diary.

Liars fabricate tales' diction of fiction.

I know who I am better find your own description.

Listen the grounds I be own you couldn't be on.

Peons be long gone before I could even ish strong arm.

Turn my back on acts without an axe to kill.

My skills carry a build like them pans cast steel.

Play feign 2

Without emotion ignite what I write in blindsight.

Whether morning, afternoon or evening the night life.

Half past nine cheap liquor or fine wine.

Sound of music in my mind the guard always aligned.

Cross multiple angles pen-game will thank you.

Fourth dimension energy recycled fifth off the ankle.

Fly high with speed as I'm flash or mercury.

Feel what is to be as I'm moving off high degrees.

No puppet master to craft the inner me become fatality.

Masquerade casualties end up where dead flowers be.

What they want must be a stunt to knock me off my square.

My elevation is here with nobody inside my ear.

Thoughts come alive from inside my hyper drive.

I'm in and out of space don't touch the king's vibe.

Keep up on the one, two don't be the one I run through.

Tell me if you want to, I got something to haunt you.

Eyes inside my eyes

If the windows are tinted and my vision become blur.

It's not only about me when I'm connected with her.

Believing in a man who chose to give apart of him.

Before relationship begin, we starting off as friends.

Hugging the heart within the external of my skin.

It's a Atterbury spin dry and cycle wash in ton.

Oh, maybe silent so defiant against the norm.

Some fall a victim of whatever's gone don't even mourn.

Celebration of life memories are deep and held.

Before you understand it's best to know JoeL.

See I look learn and listen playing my own position.

Posted up in my kitchen cooking while others be different.

Smiles last longer than deception when you are truthful.

Enjoying the most beautiful and wonderful suitable.

Companionship that gcts a lift instead of drift.

Why be a curse on a verse when you can be a nice gift.

Four fifty ascensions

Here we both are moving outside what's traditional.

Undressing each other as we stare inside our moment.

Last thoughts known was the kiss within the kiss.

Activation executed the touch open the channel.

Standing behind her nice, rounded ass holding her waistline.

Slowly breathing as I'm speaking in a tone that brings a chill.

Hands go lower touching her clitoris place my mouth on her earlobe.

Small sounds begin as she back herself close upon me.

Stronger with the embrace as we now face to face.

Lay her down without asking as I taste her with sharpness.

Now that I have her moist shh do not speak.

I am already at attention as I spread her legs apart.

Hahahahaha our eyes search each other's thoughts.

I'm thinking she about to get lost as I'm placing part of myself in her.

Hmm after a while I can feel the heat become higher.

Turn her over without expectation stroking more with intensity.

My name is my name as she brings her all to me.

Licking up the middle of her back filling her mind with ecstasy.

Here my dear let me kiss your joyful tears.

Share a French connection as we feel each other's air.

I'm inside another, wave!

The guard stay moving observation is A1.

Don't matter where I'm from you don't really want none.

Mind yours I mind mines intuition strong enough.

Break any cuffs what I trust is on the low, hush.

Speaking never over reading energy of the opposite.

Go tell Rosalind I won't be depositing my dominance.

Protect every step that I take even if I do slide.

The high inside my drive reach miles when doors fly.

Open is the toll on and off the road, success.

When you hate on the blessed congratulations, no rest!

Chest stays low never pumped only leveled.

I'm a soldier who got older and showed the cobras.

Ain't it funky

Brothers sleep on the archive I'm a real element.

Some not even revenants the streets need evidence.

Where I come from some know it's sixty-forty.

Detectives never saw me a snitch help them toss me.

Inside them steel bars because you think I go hard.

Whip come out of park when my grind begins to start.

Walked out the spaceship color of these racist.

Harlem taught me patience writing lines basic.

Coward people wasted my back to many places.

So many crooked faces hiding around mazes.

Elevation sky high evolving through the years good.

Now meet the author and poet of nineteen books.

My style is land of lake creating bars of butter.

Flow like no other alone time is covered.

Two thousand seventeen to this twenty-twenty two.

Watch the man behind hands bring forth something new.

only time in your life

Here we are placing one another in each other's thoughts.

This is a special dedication to you that I give unwrapped.

Hope this brings happiness and joy into your day.

When I know hearing your voice sends a smile upon my face.

It's the sound also the words that show sincerity and truth.

Everywhere that I be your image reflects us.

Reading your words and responding is a vibe nobody has.

Because as we move in unison it's a story untold coming soon.

Aww this is a holding hand hug and kiss creation.

As we look and search each other's soul for that place to keep comfort.

What's the number that we see or the signs that we see.

There's a place for you and me between space and blind time.

My cousins New York

Peace and love to Danielle, Michelle, and Antoinette.

Thank you for being the cousins that you are to me

always showing love.

Much appreciation you beautiful sisters.

Love you all

Special shout-out to the members of

VERSES & VIBES crew.

I appreciate and respect you all for allowing me to be a part of
your crew.

Besides I enjoy doing poetry corner westside connection with you
EB&FLO and Mz.DREA THE POET

LETS TALK PRESENTS POETRY CORNER
TUESDAYS 8PM EST.
poetry
HOST
KING
ATTERBURY

ON AIR
LET'S TALK PRESENTS
KING'S POP-UP
Producer
Q FORD
ALTERNATING
THURSDAY
8pm EST.
EVERY
HOST
JW
ATTERBURY

KING AND QUEEN QUARTERS
WITH HOSTS
KING ATTERBURY & QUEEN
SIMMONS
poetry
E.R
THE 4REAL ENTERTAINMENT NETWORK

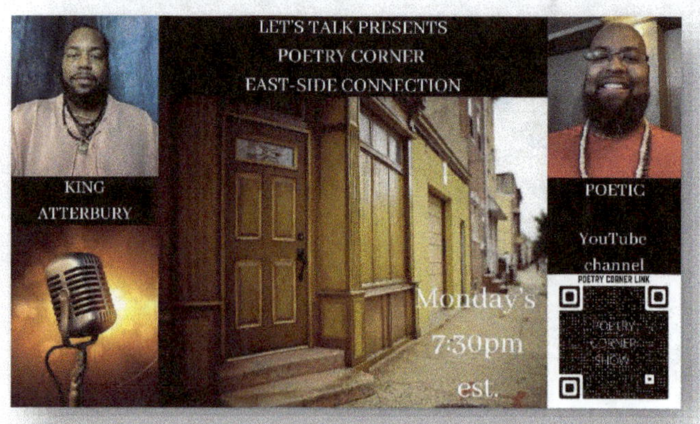

LET'S TALK PRESENTS
POETRY CORNER
EAST-SIDE CONNECTION
KING
ATTERBURY
POETIC
YouTube
channel
POETRY CORNER LINK
POETRY CORNER SHOW
Monday's
7:30pm
est.

POETRY CORNER WESTSIDE CONNECTION
PRODUCER:Q FORD
@QMIDTOWN
HOST:KING ATTERBERRY
@KING_ATTERBERRY_INK
CO-HOST: A. LEE
@MS.DREA_THEPOET
SPECIAL GUEST: ED&FLO
@TOMORROW_ REMINISCE
THURSDAY'S
8PM PCT 11PM EST

Author and poet king atterbury
YOUTUBE: KING ATTERBERRY INK

KING ATTERBERRY INK
MR. JW ATTERBURY
CONTENT CREATOR
AUTHOR & POET
609-408-3396
www.kingatterberry.com

AUTHOR + POET
JOEL
WASHINGTON ATTERBURY
FOCUS ON THE WORLD
THROUGH SPIRITUAL
ASSESSMENT!

Big shout out to my cousin QUINTEN FORD

**Cuz, we are here! POETRY CORNER all
the way to another galaxy.**

Joel
Washington
Atterbury